LIVING IN THE WILD: BIG CATS

Charlotte Guillain

Raintree is an imprint of Capstone Global Library Limited, a company incorporated in England and Wales having its registered office at 7 Pilgrim Street, London, EC4V 6LB – Registered company number: 6695582

www.raintreepublishers.co.uk
myorders@raintreepublishers.co.uk

Text © Capstone Global Library Limited 2014
First published in hardback in 2014
The moral rights of the proprietor have been asserted.

Edited by Clare Lewis and Adrian Vigliano
Designed by Tim Bond
Original illustrations © HL Studios
Picture research by Tracy Cummins
Originated by Capstone Global Library Ltd
Printed and bound in China

ISBN 978 1 406 27346 5
17 16 15 14 13
10 9 8 7 6 5 4 3 2 1

A full catalogue record for this book is available from the British Library.

Acknowledgments

The author and publisher are grateful to the following for permission to reproduce copyright material:
AP Photo p. 41 (UC Davis); Ben Battles p. 37; Getty Images pp. 6 (Guy Crittenden), 7 (Tui De Roy), 12 (Terry A Parker), 13 (Amy & Chuck Wiley/Wales), 20 (James Michael Kruger), 22, 35 (Thomas Kitchin & Victoria Hurst), 23 (William Ervin), 24 (Don Johnston), 25 (Norbert Rosing), 27 (Kevin Schafer), 28 (Danihernanz), 33 (Ronald Wittek), 39 (National Geographic), 42 (Drew Rush), 43 (Daniel J Cox), 45 (Konrad Wothe); Shutterstock pp. 5 (Dennis Donohue), 9 (Stu Porter), 15, 19, 29 (Dennis Donohue), 18 (Pictureguy), 31 (8690472142); Superstock pp. 11 (Gerard Lacz Images), 17 (Minden Pictures).

Cover photograph of a mountain lion reproduced with permission of Getty Images (Panoramic Images).

We would like to thank Michael Bright for his invaluable help in the preparation of this book.

Every effort has been made to contact copyright holders of any material reproduced in this book. Any omissions will be rectified in subsequent printings if notice is given to the publisher.

Disclaimer

Contents

Some words are shown in bold, **like this**. You can find out what they mean by looking in the glossary.

What are big cats?

A silent hunter slinks unseen across a rocky landscape. It spots a deer grazing down below. The **predator** creeps closer until it crouches on a rock just behind its prey. Then, with one powerful leap, the cat seizes its victim, pulling it to the ground and breaking its neck. The puma has caught its latest meal.

Pumas are mammals that are often included in a group called big cats. The general term 'big cat' refers to wild cats that are significantly larger than small wild cats, such as lynx, serval, and ocelot. These larger cats include pumas, jaguars, cheetahs, lions, tigers, leopards, snow leopards, and clouded leopards. However, sometimes the term big cat is used more specifically to refer to large wild cats that can roar: lions, tigers, leopards, and jaguars. Pumas are unable to roar but do make a range of other sounds.

The wider group of big cats that includes pumas shares the following characteristics:

- They are all above a certain size.
- They are all carnivores.
- None of them is hunted for food by another predator once they reach adulthood.

Big cats live in different **habitats** around the world, ranging from the rainforests of South America to African grasslands and the mountains of Southeast Asia. Some, such as leopards, can climb trees while others, such as jaguars, are strong swimmers. Lions are the most social cats, living in groups called prides. All big cats have colouring or patterns on their fur that help to conceal them as they hunt.

Pumas are solitary and beautiful wild animals.

What are pumas?

Pumas are the second largest cat in North and South America, after the jaguar. They have long, slender bodies with a flexible spine and a very long tail that is about a third of the cat's total length. Pumas have muscular rear legs that give them the power to jump great distances. Their paws are large, with sharp, curved, **retractable** claws. Their heads are relatively small and broad, with short, round ears and large eyes.

Adult pumas have unpatterned coats, which range from a sandy yellow to a brownish red. Some pumas have silvery-grey fur. Their underside is a paler colour and the sides of their muzzle and tips of their tails are darker. Their hair is short and roughly textured.

Pumas that live close to the **equator** tend to be smaller than those that live further north and south. This is because the cats living in cooler climates tend to eat larger **prey** than those in tropical habitats.

A puma's back legs are bigger and more powerful than its front legs.

Male pumas are larger than females. The largest males can weigh up to 100 kilograms (220 pounds), the average being about 62 kilograms (136 pounds). Male pumas tend to be around 1.2 metres (4 feet) long, with a tail of about 75 centimetres (2.5 feet). Females are shorter and reach an average weight of about 42 kilograms (93 pounds). Their body length ranges between 90 and 150 centimetres (3 to 5 feet), while their tails are up to 79 centimetres (32 inches) long.

RECORD HOLDER

Pumas have many different names and are also known as cougars, mountain lions, panthers, catamounts, and painters. This cat holds the Guinness world record for the mammal with the most names!

How are pumas classified?

Classification groups

Classification triangles are used to show how each living thing is **classified**. Towards the bottom of the triangle each group contains fewer and fewer members. For example, there are fewer animals in the order Carnivora (carnivores) than there are in the class Mammalia (mammals), and so on.

Pumas are in the family Felidae, which includes all cats, large and small, wild and domesticated.

Living things are given a Latin name, such as *Puma concolor*, so they have a single name rather than many different names in different languages. The puma is also a member of the sub-family Felinae, and so is related to all the smaller cats, such as the cheetah, lynx, and the domestic pet cat.

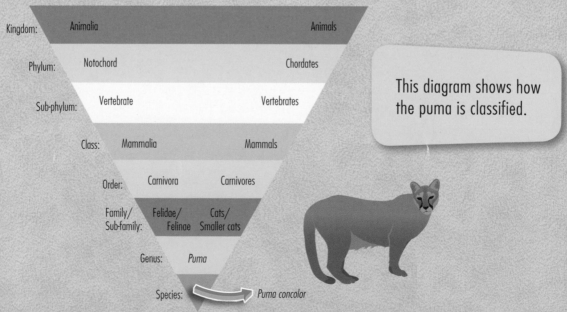

Kingdom:	Animalia	Animals
Phylum:	Notochord	Chordates
Sub-phylum:	Vertebrate	Vertebrates
Class:	Mammalia	Mammals
Order:	Carnivora	Carnivores
Family/ Sub-family:	Felidae/ Felinae	Cats/ Smaller cats
Genus:	*Puma*	
Species:		*Puma concolor*

This diagram shows how the puma is classified.

Although pumas are sometimes called mountain lions, a puma looks quite different from an African lion (such as the one shown here). Lions are bigger and more powerful.

SUBSPECIES

Scientists think there are six subspecies of puma. It's possible that the Florida panther is a seventh subspecies, but there are very few of these cats left in the wild. Some subspecies are flourishing in many areas but others are endangered.

Where do pumas live?

All wild animals live in habitats. A habitat is a place where an animal has everything it needs to survive, including food, water, and shelter. Some big cats live in very particular habitats, but pumas are able to thrive in many different types of surrounding.

Wide-ranging cat

Pumas can be found living across a huge range, from Canada, down the west of the United States, and on through Central and South America to the south of Chile. They make their home in 28 different countries.

This widespread geographical range means that pumas live in a variety of habitats. These include pine forest, tropical forest, grasslands, swamps, mountains, and cold desert regions at a high altitude. Pumas are very good at adapting to new surroundings and although they prefer to live where there are plenty of plants to provide cover, they are also able to live in more open landscapes. A puma needs to live where there is plenty of prey and enough cover, such as rocks, caves, and trees to provide shelter.

FALLING NUMBERS

Pumas may still live over a huge geographical range but they are found in far fewer places today than in the past. Pumas used to live from the west coast to the east coast of North America, and as far south as southern Argentina and Chile. Today, however, they are limited to a smaller range, with none left in eastern North America apart from very few pumas found in Florida.

This wild, rocky landscape is a perfect puma habitat.

Use this map to see where pumas live around the world.

Canada

United States

N
W E
S

Atlantic Ocean

Mexico
Belize
Guatemala
Honduras
Costa Rica
Panama
Nicaragua
Ecuador
Peru
Venezuela
Colombia
Guyana
Suriname
French Guiana
Brazil
Bolivia

Pacific Ocean

Chile
Argentina
Uruguay

Key
Where pumas live

What adaptations help pumas survive?

All animals have **adaptation**s that enable them to live in a habitat in a particular way. These adaptations have gradually developed in a **species** over thousands of years.

Fast and flexible

Pumas can't run as fast as lots of the prey it hunts, but it can sprint over a short distance once it has got close enough to its victim. A puma can reach speeds of around 80 kilometres per hour (50 miles per hour) as it runs. Its long, flexible spine is an adaptation that allows the puma to change direction quickly as it chases prey and dodges obstacles in its path.

Pumas are adapted to be able to hunt prey successfully in the range of habitats where they are found.

Pumas can jump 12 metres (40 feet) while running and 6.1 metres (20 feet) up or down a slope.

Leaping cat

Pumas have large paws and especially strong back legs. This adaptation gives them the power to run in short bursts of high speed and to leap over a long distance. This leaping power enables them to jump onto prey. A puma can also bound up into trees and can jump 5.5 metres (18 feet) down from a tree to the ground. Its strong front paws also help it to climb and swim when it needs to.

LONG TAIL

In proportion to its body, the puma's tail is very long. It helps the puma to balance as it moves quickly and lands after a jump. The puma carries its heavy tail in a U-shape, curving down from its body towards the ground and back up again.

Teeth and claws

Like other predators, pumas have adaptations that help them to kill prey effectively. A puma's teeth and claws are the tools it uses to kill its victims.

A puma has sharp, retractable claws. There are five claws on its front paws and four on the rear paws.

Inside a puma's powerful, muscular jaws is a set of deadly teeth. It has very long, curved canine teeth in the top and bottom of its mouth, which grip onto prey. The special teeth at the back of its jaw, called carnassial teeth, cut and rip flesh as the puma eats.

Sharp senses

A puma's senses are also adapted to help it hunt and keep away from danger. It has large eyes positioned on the front of its head, giving the puma **binocular vision** that enables it to judge distances accurately. This is crucial when timing when to pounce on unsuspecting prey. Pumas have a wide range of vision, too. They are also able to see very well in the dark and at dusk because their eyes are able to open especially wide to let in more light and reflect it back to give stronger vision.

Pumas also have a good sense of hearing. In the dark, this helps them to locate prey that can't easily be seen. They can even move their ears in different directions when they hear a sound to get more information. Pumas can hear a wide range of frequencies, which means they can hear the high-pitched squeaks of small prey as well as the deeper sounds made by larger prey.

A puma's eyes, ears, and nose all work together perfectly to help it hunt prey.

15

Camouflage

Like other big cats, pumas rely on **camouflage** to keep them concealed as they stalk their prey. A puma's sandy-coloured coat helps to keep it hidden in sandy desert, rocky terrain, and in dry grass. A puma can sit high on a rock or on a tree branch and look out for prey while remaining completely unseen. This adaptation is crucial for getting close enough to a victim to be able to leap out and catch it in one pounce or after a short chase. A puma's camouflaged colouring also helps to hide it from danger.

Flexible feline

One of the puma's most useful adaptations is the fact that it is able to live in many different habitats and environments and hunt many different types of prey. Because a puma can adapt to its surroundings, it is less likely to be affected by any changes to any one species of prey. Animals like this are called **generalist** species.

FLEXIBLE CATS

Scientists studying pumas in Big Bend National Park in Texas, USA, observed a change in the cats' diet. Pumas in the park had fed mostly on deer but in the early 1980s the number of deer in the park fell dramatically. The pumas were not affected, because they were able to switch their main diet to peccaries, rabbits, and hares. However, female pumas that were caring for their young needed larger prey such as deer. For pumas to be able to breed successfully, large prey needs to be available for them.

Pumas are shy and solitary cats, so it suits them to be able to stay hidden as much as possible.

Typical diet

Wherever they are available, deer are likely to be a puma's preferred prey.

In western North America, mule deer are mostly eaten by pumas, while in Florida white-tailed deer are more common. Their diet can also include young moose, elk, and caribou, but they will eat smaller animals such as rabbits, opossums, birds, ground squirrels, peccaries, raccoons, and skunks. In South America, pumas tend to eat these smaller animals more often. Pumas have been known to eat other carnivores, too, such as coyotes, bobcats, and even other pumas. They will stalk and kill farm animals if there is not enough prey in the wild.

A white-tailed deer raises its tail to alert other deer if danger is nearby.

After a kill, a puma will drag its prey to a safe place before eating. This muscular cat can move prey that weighs up to seven times as much as it does.

Hunting

Pumas usually hunt at night or during dawn or dusk, which makes them **crepuscular** (active in early morning and early evening). When hunting larger prey, pumas stalk their victim until they are close enough to leap onto its back. They are able to creep up to prey almost completely silently as their rear paws step into the footprints made by the forepaws. This helps stop a stalking puma from stepping on a twig or anything else it can't see that might make a noise and alert its prey. Once a puma has leapt out and caught hold of its prey, it kills it by breaking its neck with a bite at the base of the skull.

Pumas will often eat a large amount in one feeding session.

Feeding

Pumas can go for several days without eating. A puma usually slices open its prey using its claws and eats the heart, lungs, and liver first. These organs are more nutritious for the puma than other body parts. By eating these parts first, the puma ensures it gets the most from a kill if it is disturbed later and has to abandon its prey.

Puma food web

All animals have to eat plants or other animals to live and they, in turn, may be eaten by other animals. This is called a **food chain**. The energy in a food chain starts with the sun. Plants use the sun's energy to make food and are called **producers**. Animals are called **consumers** because they consume (eat) plants or other animals. Animals that eat plants for energy (herbivores) make up the next link in the food chain. These include many of the animals eaten by pumas. Carnivores make up the next link in the food chain, getting their energy from the animals they eat. Many connected food chains make up a **food web**.

Puma

Coyote

White-tailed deer

Rabbit

Squirrel

Plants

In a food web, the arrows go from the plant or animal being eaten to the animal that eats it. In this food web, white-tailed deer, rabbits and squirrels eat plants. Pumas eat white-tailed deer, rabbits and squirrels. They also eat the coyotes that eat the rabbits and squirrels.

What is a puma's life cycle?

An animal's life cycle is the stages it goes through from birth to death. A puma's life cycle goes through three main stages: birth, youth, and adulthood. Pumas reach adulthood when they are old enough to **reproduce** and have young themselves.

Meeting and mating

Pumas **mate** all year round, although in the north it tends to happen from December to March. Males and females don't mix at other times, staying within their own **territory**. A male puma will find a female who is ready to mate by following the sounds she makes. She will also use **scent-marking** to show she is looking for a mate. Male pumas are usually about three years old when they are ready to mate, while females are around two and a half years old.

Male and female pumas stay together for up to ten days while they mate. After this, the male leaves and has nothing to do with the kittens when they are born.

Birth of kittens

A female is **pregnant** for up to 96 days, before giving birth to kittens, sometimes called cubs. She prepares a sheltered den before giving birth to between one and six kittens. The newborn kittens are tiny, weighing between 226 and 453 grams (8 to 16 ounces). Their fur is spotted and they are completely helpless, needing their mother to feed and protect them in the den until they are stronger. Puma kittens are born with their eyes and ears shut and they start to open after about ten days. Their teeth also start to grow then, too.

Puma kittens are between two and four times as heavy as a domestic cat's kitten.

Camouflaged kittens

Puma kittens are born with blue eyes, spotted fur, and dark rings on their tails. Their patterned fur blends in with dappled light and fallen leaves. After about nine months, the spots start to blend together and fade until, around the age of two years, their fur becomes one colour and the puma is an adult. Their eyes start to change colour at around four months of age and turn a brownish-gold by the time they are fully grown.

DR MAURICE HORNOCKER

Dr Maurice Hornocker is a scientist who has studied big cats around the world for decades. He is an expert on pumas and as part of his work he has been involved in the monitoring of puma kitten **litters** in Idaho, USA. This research has helped us to understand what young pumas need to survive to adulthood.

Kittens' colouring helps to camouflage them when they are especially vulnerable.

Not having a single den is one way a mother puma keeps her kittens safe from threats.

Kitten development

Like other mammals, puma kittens feed on their mother's milk. They live on this for around 40 days and gain weight very quickly. After about six weeks, the kittens are ready to leave the den. After this, they travel with their mother, who makes **daybeds** for her young wherever they stop. These daybeds are places where kittens can rest and be protected from the weather and danger. They can be found in caves, in the faces of cliffs, or in forested areas, where they tend to be in bushes or under fallen tree trunks. Small kittens are vulnerable to other predators, such as male pumas, coyotes, bears, and eagles.

Learning to hunt

Puma kittens start to play with each other from an early age, when their teeth start to grow. For all cats, playing is an important way of learning how to hunt. Puma kittens start to go out hunting with their mother from the age of about 8 weeks. When she has made a kill, the kittens play as well as feed. They stalk and pounce on each other, and pounce on the dead prey. As they grow and become better at stalking, the kittens start to hunt alone. They will keep coming together with their mother and siblings to share feeds until they are ready to move to their own territory and live alone. This can be from the age of six months, but female pumas often care for their kittens for between one and two years.

All pumas need their own territory to ensure they get all the food, water, and shelter they need to live. When kittens leave their mother, they have to travel far enough to find their own territory, away from their mother's space. Young females can travel between 9 and 140 kilometres (5 to 86 miles) away from their mother, while young males move further away. A male kitten that is leaving its mother can travel as far as 250 kilometres (155 miles) away. It may take a while for a young puma to establish its own territory, or **home range**. It can be difficult if other pumas are already present and defend their space against the newcomer.

Cat	Lifespan in the wild
Cheetah	around 12 years
Lion	around 15 years
Jaguar	around 15 years
Leopard	around 15 years
Puma	around 20 years
Tiger	around 20 years

This chart shows the lifespan of some big cats in the wild.

Puma kittens learn the skills of hunting from an early age.

How do pumas behave?

Adult pumas live alone apart from a few days when males and females meet during mating or when a female puma is caring for her cubs. A single puma's home range can be very large as these predators travel great distances as they hunt. A female puma's home range is usually around 140 square kilometres (54 square miles) and can overlap with another female's home range without causing conflict. Male pumas have much larger home ranges that can be around 280 square kilometres (108 square miles). A male's home range usually overlaps with the home ranges of a couple of females but not with other male pumas.

Pumas tend to be most active at night and are most likely to hunt in the early morning or evening, when their prey is most active.

Pumas are solitary animals most of the time.

Marking a home range

Pumas that have established their own home range use markings to let other pumas know it is their territory. They mark the boundaries of their space by scratching trees and fallen trunks. Pumas might also push leaves, dirt, or pine needles into a pile with their paws to mark their territory. They then leave **urine** or **faeces** where they have scraped, so other cats can smell that they have been there.

RESIDENT OR TRANSIENT?

A puma that has its own home range is known as a **resident**. A puma that doesn't have its own territory, either because it is young and hasn't established one yet or because it has lost its home range to an intruder, is called a **transient**. It is much harder for transients to find the prey they need to survive.

A DAY IN THE LIFE OF A PUMA

A puma's day is split between sleeping, resting, and hunting. A female puma might spend much of the night roaming across her home range, marking her boundaries and searching for prey. Around dawn, she starts to stalk prey, creeping up until she is close enough to pounce and make a quick kill. After quickly eating part of the prey, she might then take some meat back to the daybed where her kittens are hidden. The kittens will feed both on the meat and on their mother's milk. If the prey is large, she might hide what's left and return to it for up to four days.

Playing and sleeping

As the day goes on, the female puma and her kittens sleep, rest, play, and **groom** each other. A puma's tongue is covered with tiny hooks that help to remove dirt and debris from their coats as they groom themselves. Puma kittens wrestle and chase each other as they learn the business of hunting.

Hunting

As night starts to draw in, the mother puma takes her kittens back to the daybed. She might carry them one by one in her mouth, holding them gently between her jaws. Then a puma that hasn't already hunted that day might go out looking for prey or roam its home range to check that no transient pumas have travelled through. Some of the night might be spent resting before the next day begins.

Sleeping and grooming are important parts of the day for a puma.

TACKLING INTRUDERS

If a male resident puma comes across a transient puma in its territory, they will probably fight. This can result in one of the pumas being killed or driven off the territory for good. Female pumas tend to be more tolerant of intruders in their home range.

How intelligent are pumas?

It is hard for scientists to accurately identify and measure intelligence in animals. Wild animals rely on their **instincts** as much as what we know as intelligence to survive. However, we think pumas show intelligent behaviour in the way they communicate.

Communication

Although pumas usually live alone, they are remarkably good at communicating with each other. They do this using sounds, smells, and touch.

Puma kittens make a whistling, chirpy sound when they want their mother. Adults can make hissing, growling, and mewing sounds and will purr when they feel safe and contented. A male and female that are looking to mate often make a loud wailing noise that sounds a bit like a human scream.

Touch is mostly used by a mother and her kittens to communicate through grooming and by rubbing heads and cheeks with each other. Adult pumas also rub their cheeks against rocks and plants in their surroundings so that other pumas can smell their presence. Scraping and other scent-marking communicates in a similar way using smell.

Pumas are unable to roar like lions or jaguars, but they can make a wide range of other noises.

RADIO TRACKING

Scientists have gained most of the information they know about wild pumas by using radio collars. Researchers capture a puma using a tranquilizer gun and while the cat is **sedated** they attach a collar that contains a radio transmitter. The scientists can then track the animal's movements and see how often different pumas come into contact with each other.

What threats do pumas face?

Although pumas still live across a huge expanse of North and South America, their numbers have steadily been declining for centuries. When Europeans began settling on the east coast of the United States, pumas were systematically hunted and killed. By 1850, the cats were already very rare in the east of North America. Today, the Convention of International Trade in Endangered Species (CITES) registers endangered animals to alert governments, conservationists, and the public that their populations are decreasing. CITES has classified pumas as of 'Least Concern', probably because they are found across such a large geographical area. However, conservationists are concerned that puma numbers are decreasing.

KEEPING THE BALANCE

The puma is an **umbrella species**. This means it is an animal that is protected within a certain habitat to keep a balance and make sure other species survive. In places where puma numbers have dropped, the deer population has increased to the point where land has become overgrazed and ticks carried by the deer have spread disease to other animals and humans.

Habitat loss

One of the main threats to pumas is loss of their **habitat**. As the human population grows and develops, more land that is home to pumas is used for farming and building. As well as losing actual land to human development, pumas face problems when the enormous area of land they need to roam across as part of their home range is broken up so they are no longer able to travel across it all. Changes to pumas' habitats also affect the prey animals they rely on, which can result in less food for them to hunt.

Conflict with humans

As well as losing habitat, in many areas pumas are losing the main prey animals they rely on to survive because of human hunting. Where people over-hunt deer and the other large mammals pumas need as a source of food, pumas are forced to prey on livestock, such as cattle. All across their range, pumas come into conflict with farmers when they kill their animals and humans tend to respond by shooting the pumas.

Hunting

It is legal for humans to hunt pumas under certain conditions in many western US states, Canada, Mexico, and Peru. In the United States, California and Florida are the only states where the hunting of pumas is banned. In Ecuador, El Salvador, and Guyana, pumas have no protection against hunting at all. These cats are especially vulnerable to hunting because they instinctively climb into trees to escape danger, and this makes them easy to shoot. Many people perceive pumas to be dangerous to humans, particularly children, and so will shoot pumas that come near to human settlements. In reality, pumas avoid humans as much as possible and will only attack in rare circumstances. Only around 25 people have been killed by pumas in the United States in the last 100 years.

Humans hunt pumas even though they present little threat to people.

ROAD DANGER

As human populations spread closer and closer to puma territory that was once remote, pumas fail to recognize dangers such as traffic that crosses their home range. In California and Florida, many pumas are killed on roads every year.

How can people help pumas?

Luckily, pumas are protected over most of their range. Although they can be legally hunted in several regions, it is against the law to hunt pumas in most of South America and regulations limit the amount of hunting that can take place in Canada, the United States, Mexico, and Peru. As other subspecies are becoming increasingly vulnerable, more is being done to protect pumas.

Across the puma's remaining range, conservationists are working hard to preserve the animal's habitat and ensure that areas that pumas need to travel to are not cut off to them. In the Grand Teton National Park in Wyoming, the Teton Cougar Project is involved in studying puma behaviour and trying to stop people shooting pumas. Scientists have used radio collars to gather data on how pumas behave to help direct their conservation plans. The researchers have discovered that only 20 per cent of kittens survive here beyond the age when they are ready to live independently. They have also seen evidence of pumas working together to kill prey. This might be a strategy for survival as they compete against other predators such as bears and wolves in the limited space they have to hunt.

DR HOWARD QUIGLEY

Dr Howard Quigley is Director of the Teton Cougar Project and is an expert on jaguars and pumas. He became interested in wildlife after spending time camping and fishing as a boy. Through his work protecting pumas in the United States, Dr Quigley is trying to gain support for the protection of natural areas and the deer populations that live there, so pumas can roam freely. He works hard to persuade people who live alongside pumas that they are valuable to the environment.

The kitten is being checked and weighed as part of the Teton Cougar Project.

The California Cougar Project

Another initiative that has been set up by Panthera to help protect pumas is the California Cougar Project. Panthera is an organization that works to protect wild cats around the world through research, conservation activities, and education of governments and the public.

Panthera set up the California Cougar Project (CCP) in 2008 to focus on pumas living in California, the only US state other than Florida where pumas are not hunted. A large part of the project centres on finding ways for humans and pumas to live alongside each other. A lot of work has been done to conserve the pumas' habitat in California, to educate the public about the benefits of having this wild animal in the state, and to find ways to limit conflict between people and pumas. One of the key problems for pumas in California is the breaking up of their habitat, so conservationists are looking at ways to develop corridors for pumas to travel through safely from place to place.

Research

Scientists need to study pumas living both in captivity and in the wild to find out more about what these animals need to survive. Research is an important part of the work done by organizations like Panthera and the Cougar Fund. Their studies provide the evidence needed to persuade governments of the best way to protect pumas and other wild species.

KEYSTONE CAT

Pumas are a **keystone species** in California. Other than the black bear, they are the only large carnivore left in the state and the only one that only eats meat. A keystone species is a highly influential animal in a habitat and is vital in maintaining a balance through the whole of the ecosystem.

Two researchers examine a three-year-old female puma in a California state park. The puma is wearing a tracking collar to help scientists learn more about her movements.

What does the future hold for pumas?

The puma is not the most endangered big cat in the world and, given its geographical range, it could be seen to be thriving. Scientists studying pumas at the University of Minnesota, USA, have even found evidence that puma populations are developing in parts of the United States where they haven't been seen for years. Pumas have spread from the West into the Midwest, living mainly in South Dakota. This is encouraging news for everyone seeking to protect pumas living in the wild.

However, at the same time the human population is continuing to grow and spread into typical puma habitat, either destroying it completely or breaking it up in ways that make it hard for pumas to coexist with people. The number of species that pumas depend on for prey is also falling, and the cats can still be hunted in many places. Even females still caring for dependent kittens can legally be shot and killed in many places, meaning that many young kittens die before reaching adulthood.

This scientist is studying a puma kill in the mountains of Wyoming.

We can all do our part to help wild animals such as pumas.

If pumas are to survive into the future, humans need to find ways to live successfully alongside them and value the role these beautiful cats play in our shared environment. If pumas' habitats can be protected and people educated so they want to conserve these important creatures, then the puma may have a future.

Puma profile

Species:	Puma
Latin name:	*Puma concolor*
Body length:	1.2 metres (4 feet)
Tail length:	75 centimetres (2.5 feet)
Weight:	Up to 100 kilograms (220 pounds)
Habitat:	Pine forest, tropical forest, grasslands, swamps, mountains, and cold desert regions
Diet:	Deer, moose, elk, caribou, and smaller animals such as rabbits, opossums, birds, ground squirrels, peccaries, raccoons, and skunks
Number of kittens per litter:	Around one to six cubs, with three or four on average. Females are around two and a half years old when they are ready to have cubs and give birth about once every two years.
Life expectancy:	Up to 20 years

The long, curved tail helps the puma balance as it runs after prey.

The single-coloured coat provides camouflage.

Large eyes help the puma see well in the dark, and judge distances accurately.

Long back legs give the puma the power to leap long distances.

Sharp teeth and powerful jaws help the puma catch and kill prey.

Glossary

adaptation body part or behaviour of a living thing that helps it survive in a particular habitat

binocular vision using both eyes together to see

camouflage blending in with the environment to hide

classify group living things together by their similarities and differences

consumer animal that eats plants or other animals

crepuscular active in the early morning and early evening

daybed temporary den where puma kittens are hidden safely while their mother hunts

equator imaginary line that divides Earth into the northern and southern hemispheres

faeces poo

food chain sequence in which one creature eats another, which eats another, and so on

food web network of intertwined food chains

generalist species type of animal that can be flexible about where it lives and what it eats

groom clean an animal's fur

habitat type of place or surroundings that a living thing prefers to live in

home range area in which an animal usually lives

instinct natural tendency or way of behaving

keystone species top animal in a habitat

litter group of young animals born at the same time

mate spend time together to reproduce or have young

predator animal that hunts other animals for food

pregnant condition where a female animal is carrying developing young in her body

prey animal that is hunted and killed for food by another animal

producer plant in a food chain that makes food

reproduce to have offspring

resident puma with its own home range

retractable claws that pull out

scent-marking marking territory using smell

sedated put to sleep

species group of similar living things that can mate with each other

territory area of land an animal claims as its own space

transient animal without its own home range

umbrella species type of animal that is needed in a habitat to keep the balance for all other species

urine liquid waste from an animal or human

Find out more

Books
Countdown to Extinction, David Burnie (Oxford University Press, 2008)

South America's Most Amazing Animals (Animal Top Tens), Anita Ganeri (Raintree, 2009)

ZSL Big Cats, Michael Cox (Bloomsbury Childrens, 2012)

Website
BBC Nature
www.bbc.co.uk/nature/life/cougar
Visit this website to watch videos of cougars in the wild.

Organizations
The World Wildlife Fund
www.wwf.org.uk
WWF works to protect animals and nature, and needs your help! Take a look at their website and see what you can do.

The Mountain Lion Foundation
www.mountainlion.org
This organization campaigns to increase protection for pumas in the wild.

Index